DK

A DORLING KINDERSLEY BOOK

Project Editor Mary Atkinson
Art Editor Ivan Finnegan
Design Assistant Chris Drew
Deputy Managing Editor Dawn Sirett
Deputy Managing Art Editor
C. David Gillingwater
Production Josie Alabaster
Picture Research Joanne Beardwell
Photography Peter Anderson,
Dave King, and Gary Lewis
Illustrator Ellis Nadler

First published in Great Britain in 1997
by Dorling Kindersley Limited,
9 Henrietta Street, London WC2E 8PS

A CIP catalogue record for this book
is available from the British Library.

ISBN 0-7513-5510-0

Colour reproduction by Chromagraphics, Singapore
Printed and bound in Italy by L.E.G.O.

Dorling Kindersley would like to thank the following for
their kind permission to reproduce photographs:
t=top, b=bottom, c=centre, l=left, r=right

Bruce Coleman / Luiz Claudio Marigo 14-15c, 14bl, back
jacket bl, / Norman Tomalin 16cl, / Jorg & Petra Wegner 9tr;
Philip Dowell 5br; **Biofotos** / Andrew Henley 19tr; **Frank Lane
Picture Agency** / Terry Whitaker 21br; **NHPA** / Gerard Lacz
8cr, / Kevin Schafer 15br, / Martin Wendler 17tr; **Planet Earth
Pictures** / Neil Rettig Productions 6tl;
Zefa 18tl, / Michael Lees 18c, / Minden / F. Lanting 10bl.

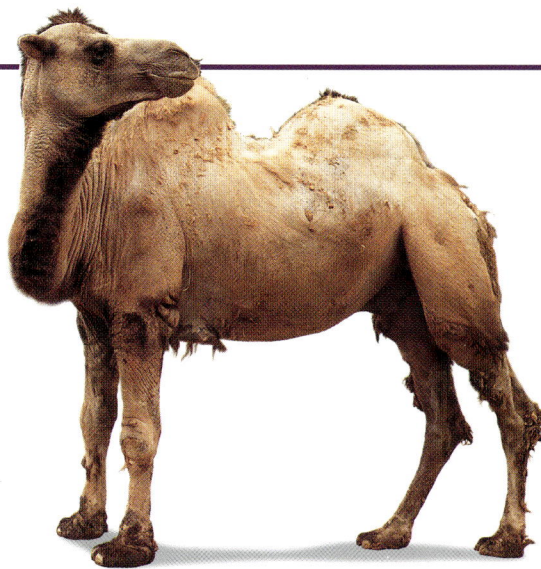

Bactrian camel
Page 12

Red kangaroo
Page 18

Baboon
Page 8

Scale
Look out for drawings like
this – they show the size of the
animals compared with people.

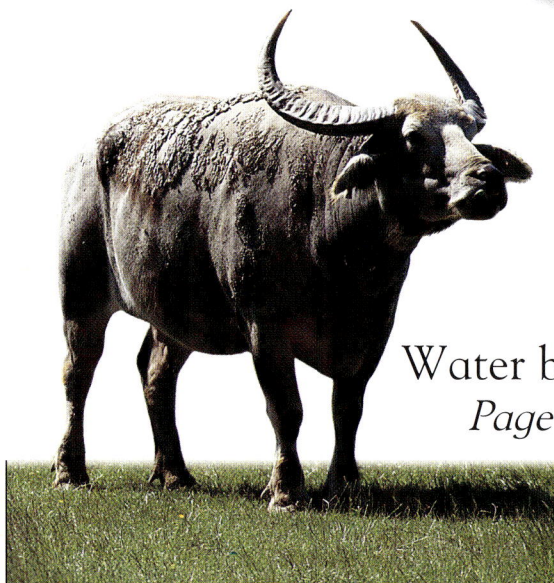

Water buffalo
Page 20

POWERFUL
BEASTS
OF THE WILD

Written by
Theresa Greenaway

Ostrich
Page 10

American
bison
Page 6

Constricting snakes
Page 16

Jaguar
Page 14

DK

Dorling Kindersley
LONDON • NEW YORK • STUTTGART • MOSCOW

American bison

Every winter, North American bison herds used to migrate south to reach warmer pastures. Some herds walked up to 500 km. It would take a fast car 5 hours to drive that far.

Early American settlers used to follow bison trails to find water. As a result, many American cities are now located on ancient bison drinking sites.

A bull can weigh up to 1 tonne. That's about the same weight as 38 seven-year-old children.

Mighty bison grow this big just by eating grass. They spend much of the day chewing. In the past, large herds roamed North America, but today, most bison are kept in reserves.

Both male and female bison have horns, but the male's are longer.

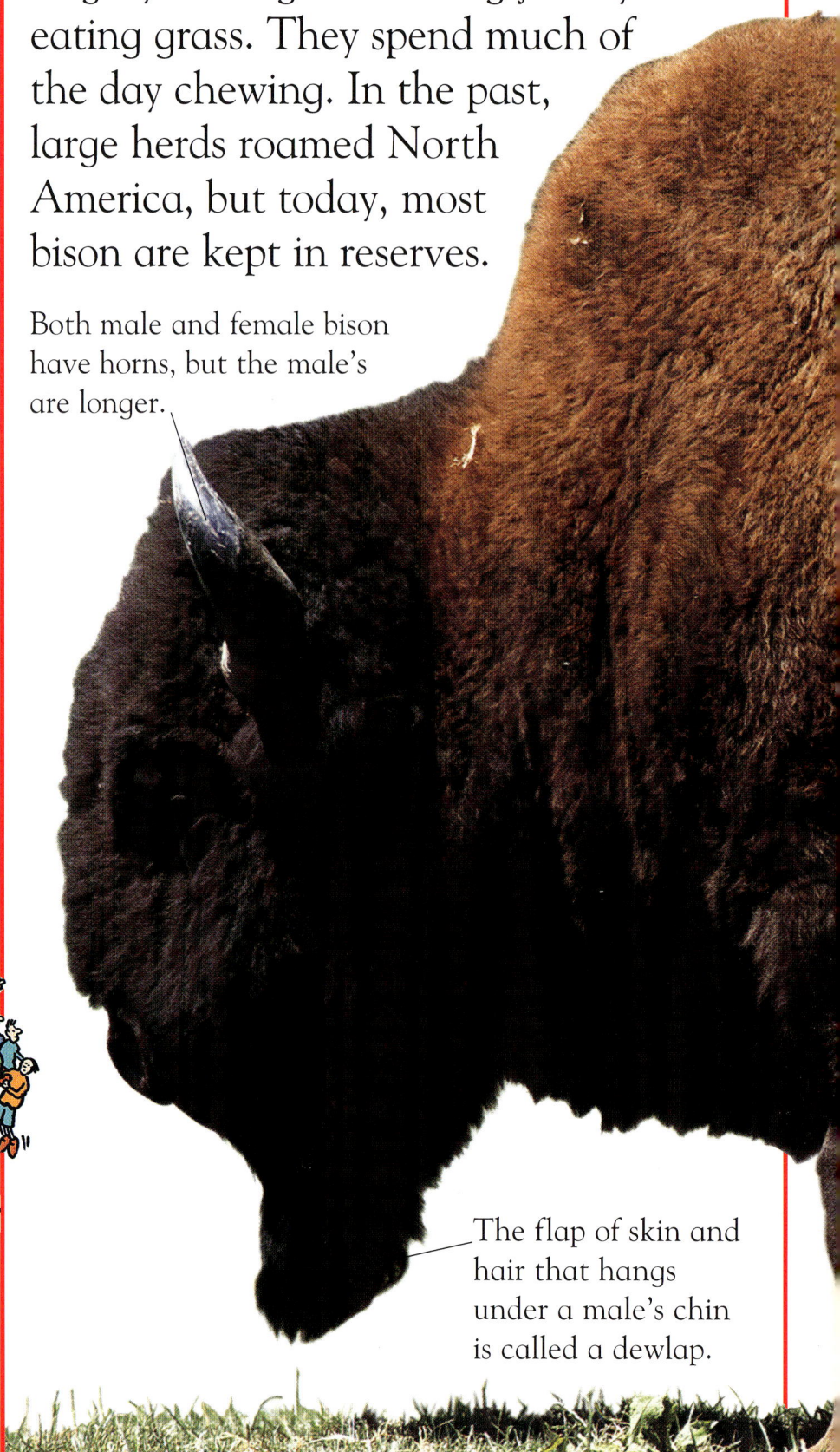

The flap of skin and hair that hangs under a male's chin is called a dewlap.

Massive, powerful shoulders help a fully grown male to overcome rivals.

The shaggy look
Bison moult in spring, shedding the soft wool that keeps them warm in winter.

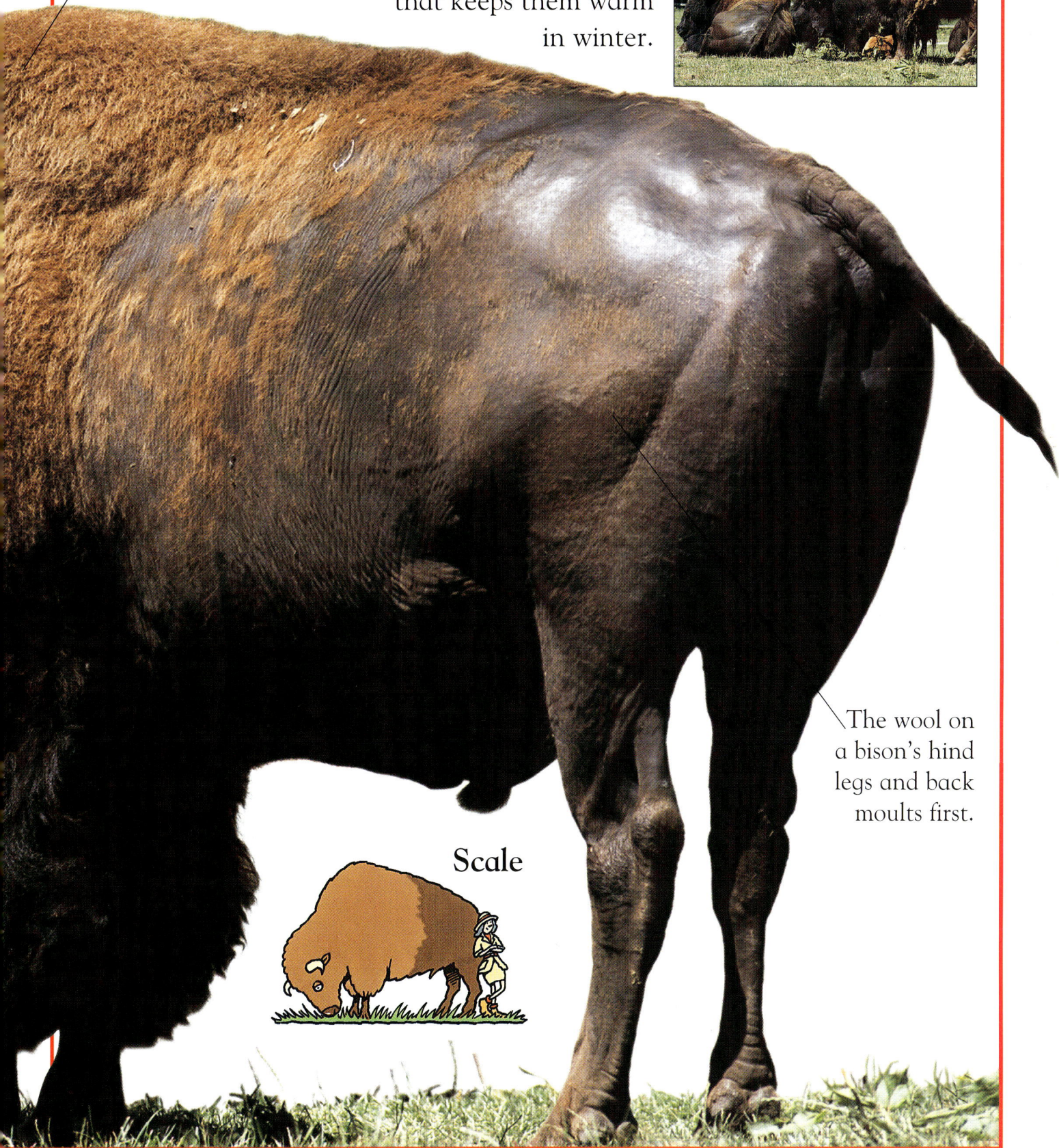

The wool on a bison's hind legs and back moults first.

Scale

When an animal **moults**, it sheds either its hair, its feathers, or a layer of skin.

7

Baboon

A hamadryas baboon has a long muzzle.

Troops of hamadryas baboons forage for food on the grassy plains and rocky crags of Ethiopia and Saudi Arabia. In these hot, dry lands, the baboons eat any leaves, fruit, or insects they can find.

male baboon

Beauty to behold
Baboons' red bottoms may look odd to us, but baboons find them very attractive.

female baboon

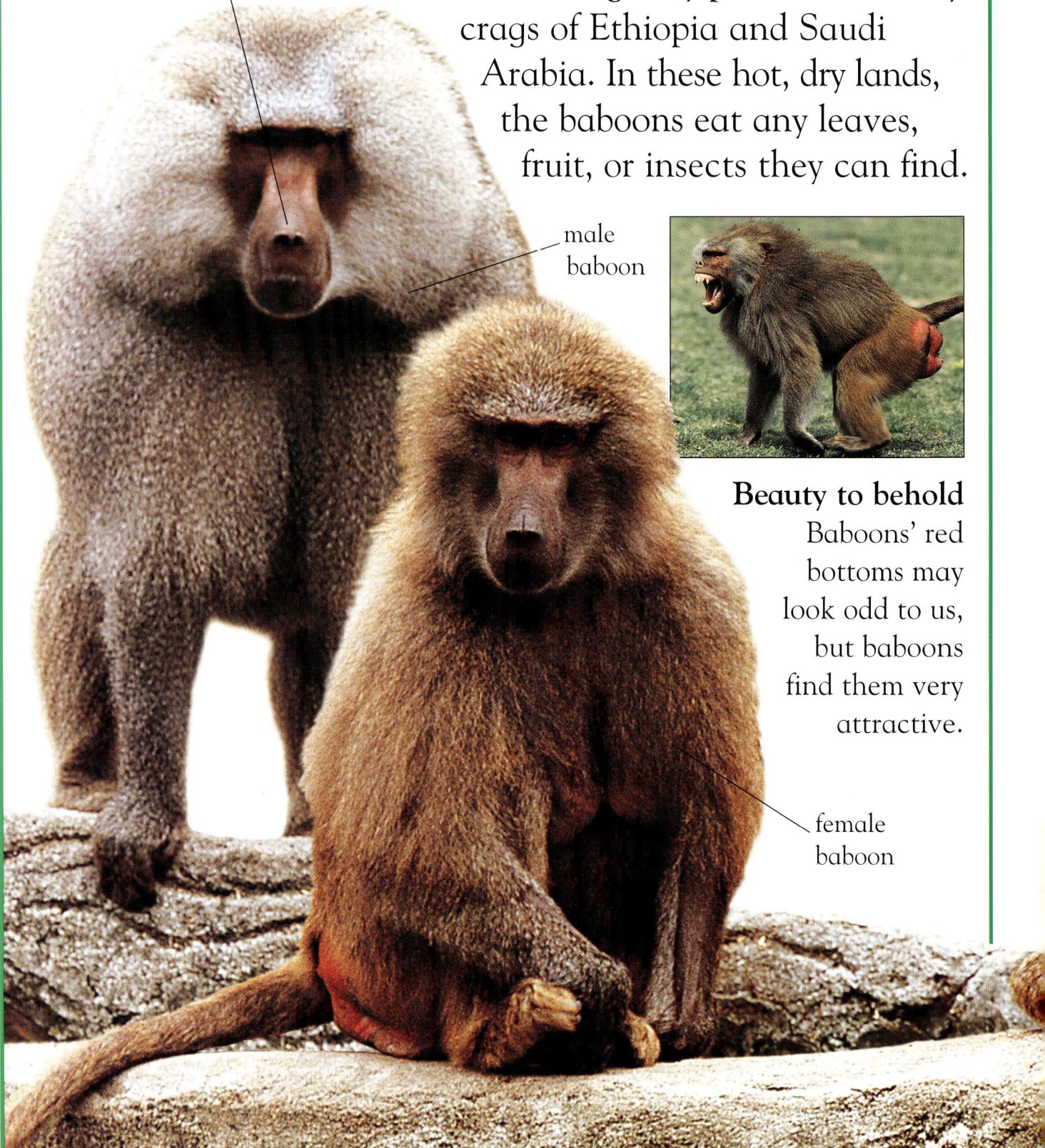

A **muzzle** is a long nose and mouth that stands out from an animal's face.

Scale

The male hamadryas baboon has a long, thick mane of silver hair.

Strike a pose

Unlike people, baboons walk about on all fours. But when they stop to groom or rest, they often sit in much the same way as we do.

Armed to the teeth

A baboon's large, sharp canine teeth are often used just to make threats, but, when necessary, they can be used to fight.

AMARING FACTS

Long ago, in ancient Egypt, the hamadryas baboon was known as the sacred baboon. It represented the moon god, Thoth.

Baboons throw stones at predators, such as leopards – but only from a safe distance. They also bark menacingly at these enemies.

Canine teeth have sharp, pointed ends. They are usually used for tearing food.

Ostrich

These long-legged, long-necked birds sprint around the hot, dry African plains. It's not surprising that they can't fly – they weigh up to 150 kg, the same weight as two grown men.

An ostrich's neck is nearly half as long as its whole body.

Beep beep
Ostriches can run faster than any other bird. They sometimes reach 72 km per hour, which is faster than a racehorse.

Ostriches are farmed for their long, fluffy wing and tail feathers and for their meat.

Head in the sand?
An ostrich doesn't really bury its head in sand. But, when a female incubates her eggs, she lays her head down to avoid being noticed.

When a bird sits on its eggs to keep them warm, it **incubates** them.

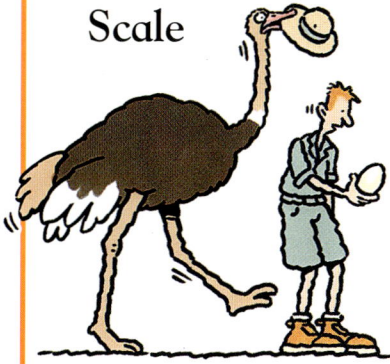

Soft down and bristles cover the ostrich's head and neck.

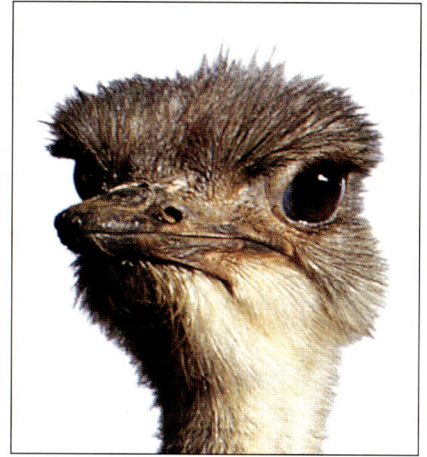

Although the ostrich is the world's largest bird, its brain is not very big. In fact, it's smaller than just one of its eyes.

Ostriches lay the biggest eggs of any bird. Each one is about the same size as 20 hens' eggs.

Suitable suits
The female's brown coat helps camouflage her when she sits on her eggs, while the male's smart black-and-white suit helps him to impress possible mates.

Ostriches have been known to swallow all sorts of strange things, including coins, combs, pieces of rope, and even an alarm clock!

An ostrich walks about on two large toes.

Camouflage colours or markings help to hide an animal in its surroundings.

Bactrian camel

Wild Bactrian camels are found only in the Gobi desert, where the summers are hot, dry, and windy. These hardy creatures cope well in this environment. They can even close their nostrils to keep out sand.

An angry camel uses its sharp combat teeth for biting, and can spit a foul-smelling liquid from its stomach.

When thirsty, a camel can drink 120 litres in just 10 minutes. That's like you drinking 360 cans of soft drink in a row.

Bactrian camels have two humps and a hairy beard. Camels with one hump are called dromedaries.

Spread-out toes

A camel's foot has two wide toes joined by a web of skin. They spread the camel's weight so that it doesn't sink into soft sand or deep snow.

Winters in the Gobi desert are freezing cold. To keep warm, the Bactrian camel grows a thick, woolly coat, which it sheds in spring.

Thick skin on the soles of the camel's feet protect it from the scorching hot sand.

An animal's surroundings, including plants and weather, make up its **environment**.

Camels store fat in their humps. They can go for long periods without food by using this source of energy.

Scale

Working animals

Camels have been domesticated for more than 4,000 years. Today, many desert people still rely on camels for transportation and use their dung as fuel.

Jaguar

Sometimes a jaguar is born with a black coat. However, in bright light, faint spots can still be seen.

Jaguars are good swimmers and like to cool down in rivers. They will sometimes hunt in water, catching unwary animals that come for a drink.

Jaguars weigh up to 158 kg. That's more than two adult people. They're the third heaviest of the big cats. Only lions and tigers weigh more.

Jaguars are fierce and powerful predators. Although they are now rare, hundreds of jaguars once roamed the jungles of South America, hunting wild pigs, tapirs, and even alligators.

Jaguars' long tails help them to balance when running or climbing.

Home territory
Jaguars live alone, fiercely guarding their territory, and the scarce prey that live in it, from other jaguars.

An animal's **territory** is an area of land that it defends from other animals.

Scale

Like other cats, a jaguar has good eyesight. It's much more likely to see you than you are to see it.

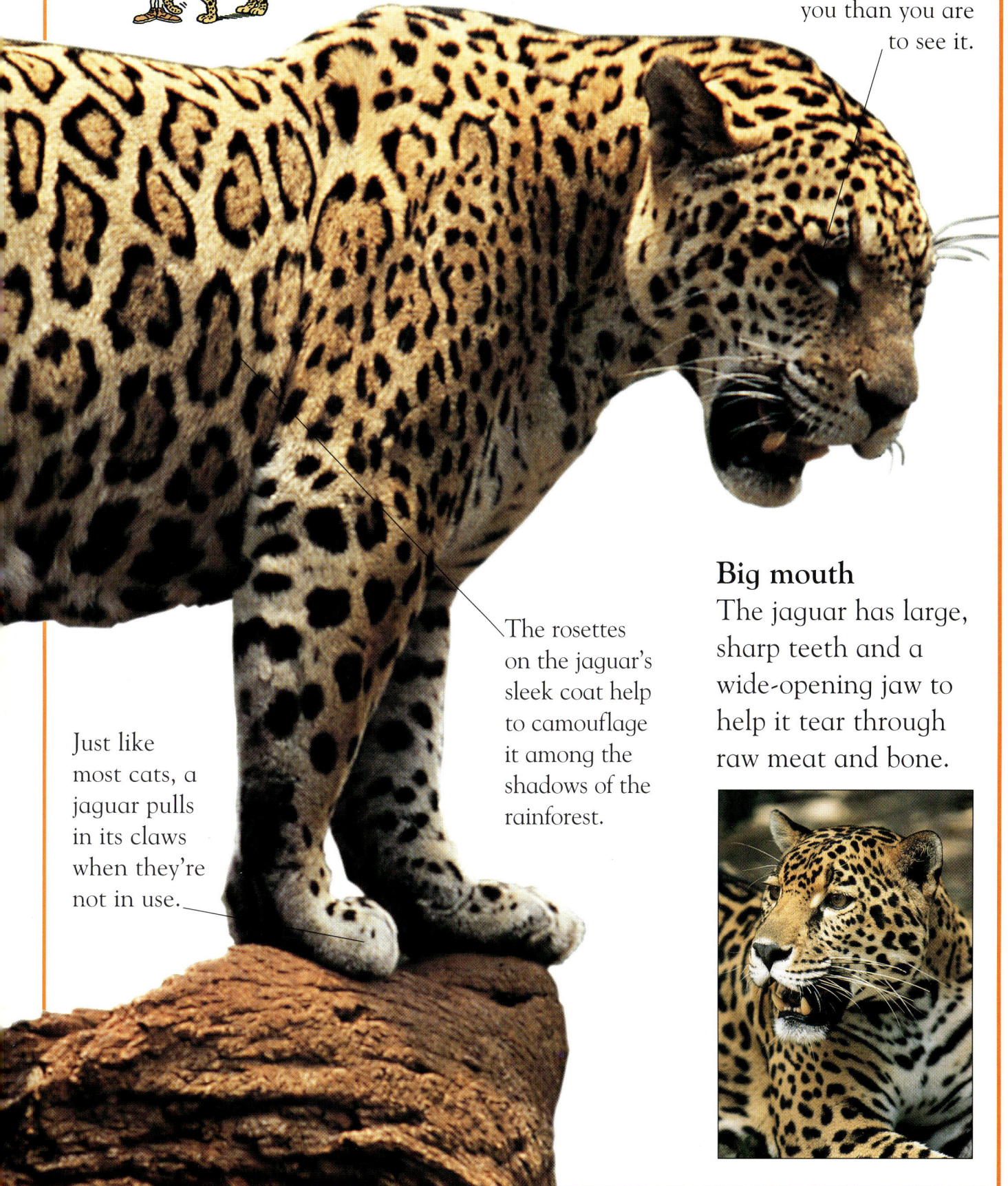

Big mouth

The jaguar has large, sharp teeth and a wide-opening jaw to help it tear through raw meat and bone.

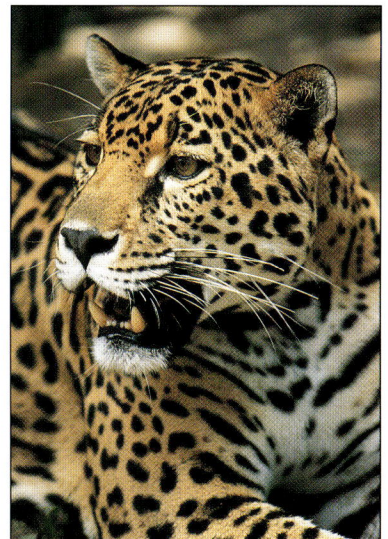

The rosettes on the jaguar's sleek coat help to camouflage it among the shadows of the rainforest.

Just like most cats, a jaguar pulls in its claws when they're not in use.

Constricting snakes

Constricting snakes, such as pythons and anacondas, are rippling masses of powerful muscles. Their prey are squeezed to death and then swallowed whole.

This python often lives near water. It swims by wriggling its body from side to side.

Burmese python

Watch out
Like many snakes, this python's camouflage pattern makes it very hard to spot.

Scale

A snake's smooth, shiny scales are hardened patches of skin.

A **constricting** snake kills its prey by squeezing it.

A tight squeeze

Anacondas often hunt in swamps or rivers. This anaconda has captured a caiman, and will suffocate it by tightening its grip.

Up to 400 pairs of ribs support a snake's one long lung.

The reticulated python is the world's longest snake. At up to 10 metres, it's even longer than a bus.

Some pythons can open their jaws wide enough to swallow an entire leopard or antelope.

A snake grips the ground with the edges of its scales to push itself forward.

Anacondas are the heaviest snakes. They can weigh 150 kg, as much as six seven-year-old children.

When an animal is unable to breathe, it **suffocates**.

17

Red kangaroo

When in danger from predators, such as dingoes, red kangaroos can leap along at a top speed of 65 km per hour. That's faster than a city car.

Red kangaroos can jump up to 3 metres into the air to make an escape. That's as high as a basketball net.

Male red kangaroos stand at 1.65 metres – about as tall as a human.

Red kangaroos are the tallest kangaroos in Australia. They can cover vast distances, bounding along on their powerful hind legs. Mobs of about ten kangaroos live together, feeding on any grass they find as they move about the dry plains.

A fully grown male kangaroo is sometimes called a "boomer".

Colour-coded coats
The older male red kangaroos have rich red coats. The females usually have duller coloured coats.

A group of kangaroos living together is called a **mob**.

Kangaroos can twist their ears around to pick up any sounds made by approaching predators.

Mobile home

Kangaroos are marsupials. A tiny newborn joey lives in its mother's pouch. Even when it's quite big, an alarmed joey will hop back into the pouch for safety.

When kangaroos fight, they box each other with their front paws.

Kangaroos have a stiff, muscular tail to balance them as they leap along.

Scale

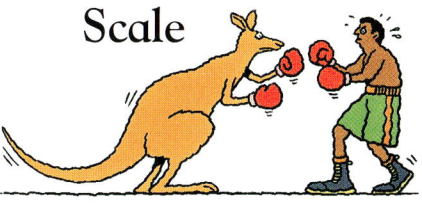

Large, strong feet push the kangaroo forward in huge leaps. They can also deliver a powerful kick.

A **marsupial** is an animal that is carried in its mother's pouch as a baby.

Water buffalo

Herds of wild water buffalo used to roam the swampy grasslands of India and Sri Lanka. Nowadays, few water buffalo are left in the wild; most pull ploughs in the wet paddy fields where rice is grown.

🐾 Water buffalo have the largest horns of all cattle. The record pair were 4.24 metres along their curve – even longer than two tall men.

🐾 A male water buffalo can weigh 1.2 tonnes. That's as much as 46 seven-year-old children!

🐾 Mighty water buffalo have few enemies. Even a tiger stands little chance against an angry bull buffalo.

Dried mud protects the water buffalo's skin from both the burning sun and insect bites.

🐾 A large group of some animals such as cattle or antelope is called a **herd**. 🐾

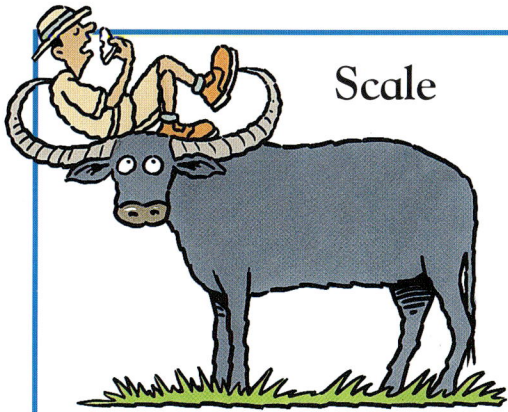

Scale

Horns aplenty

Both male and female buffalo have horns. As they grow older, their horns grow longer. They use them for defence and to settle disputes between themselves.

Water wallowers

During the heat of the day, water buffalo stay cool in muddy wallows. They come out to graze in the evening, when the temperature drops.

To **graze** means to eat the grasses growing in a grassland or field.